Evan-Moor Celebrates 25 Years of Helping Children Learn

The book you are holding in your hands is the reason **Evan-Moor Educational Publishers** was founded.

In 1977, Joy Evans and Jo Ellen Moore were team-teaching first grade in California. Many of their students lacked the language background necessary for academic success. For example, a number of them did not know concepts such as *on, under, in front of,* or *behind.* Joy and Jo Ellen decided to use art experiences as the motivator to generate language concepts. The approach worked; students readily learned new adjectives, verbs, and positional words when they were presented during the art lessons.

In 1978, they published a book entitled *Art Moves the Basics Along – Animal Units.* The book was 42 pages long and contained ten of their most popular units. Joy and Jo Ellen wrote the book. Joy illustrated the book. Joy's brother Bill wrote the forward. They had the book printed at a local printer, and all three ran around a kitchen table assembling the pages. They tried selling the book through direct mail but without great success. The book was offered to several other educational publishers, but no offers were accepted.

During this time, Joy and Jo Ellen wrote four books for Frank Schaffer Publications.

An editor at Frank Schaffer encouraged Joy, Jo Ellen, and Bill to go into business together. In July of 1979, **Evan-Moor Educational Publishers** was officially incorporated in the State of California. On September 7, 1979, **Evan-Moor** made its first sale to Mrs. Joyce M. Smith of Minneapolis, Minnesota. In our first year of existence, we entered educational publishing with a total of six titles. Among those six titles was *Art Moves the Basics Along – Animal Units.*

At **Evan-Moor**, we are proud that our products are written, edited, and tested by teachers. We focus on prekindergarten through sixth-grade materials.

About Evan-Moor Educational Publishers

Who We Are

- At Evan-Moor, we are proud that our products are written, edited, and tested by professional educators.

- Evan-Moor's materials are directed to teachers and parents of Prekindergarten through sixth-grade students.

- We address all major curriculum areas including:

reading	social studies	writing
math	thematic units	science
geography	arts & crafts	

How We Began

- In 1979, Joy Evans and Jo Ellen Moore were team-teaching first grade in a Title I school. They decided to put ideas that worked for their students into a book. They joined with Bill Evans (Joy's brother) to start Evan-Moor Educational Publishers with one book.

- Bill and Joy's parents' garage served as the warehouse and shipping facility.

- The first catalog was a folded 8 ½" x 11" sheet of paper!

Who We Became

- Evan-Moor now offers over 450 titles. Our materials can be found in over 1,500 educational and trade book stores around the world.

- We mail almost 2 million catalogs a year to schools and individual teachers.

- Our Web site www.evan-moor.com offers 24-hour service and the ability to download many of our titles.

- Evan-Moor is located in a 20,000-square-foot facility in Monterey, California, with a staff of nearly 60 professionals.

Our Mission

Now, as then, we are dedicated to helping children learn. We think it is the world's most important job, and we strive to assist teachers and parents in this essential endeavor.

Evan-Moor™
EDUCATIONAL PUBLISHERS
Helping Children Learn

ART MOVES THE BASICS ALONG

by

JOY EVANS   JO ELLEN MOORE

Congratulations on your purchase of some of the finest teaching materials in the world.

EMC 075

Evan-Moor™
EDUCATIONAL PUBLISHERS

Authors: Joy Evans and Jo Ellen Moore

For information about other Evan-Moor products,
call 1-800-777-4362 or FAX 1-800-777-4332.
Visit our Web site www.evan-moor.com.
Check the Product Updates link for supplements,
additions, and corrections for this book.

"Teaching Drawing For The Artistic Klutz And Others"
by
Evans and Moore

"I CAN'T DRAW!" This was the response we got from many of our fellow teachers when we asked them why they didn't emphasize art activities in their classrooms. One of our colleagues commented in a faculty meeting, "It was after I tried teaching my class how to draw a doggie that I seriously questioned how I could have earned a liberal <u>ARTS</u> degree!" Unfortunately, art has become a rainy day activity for many of us, when it could be a vital part of our elementary curriculum.

Many teachers also feel discouraged because their students lack artistic confidence. "I can't draw....they can't draw. Maybe we can just stick to crayons and string pull paintings again this year." NONSENSE! You can draw... they will learn to draw. There's no big trick to it.

Using the techniques in this book, we have found that even first grade students become confident and comfortable with a wide variety of art projects. Fear of failure (for you and the student) can be replaced with the excitement and joy of a successfully completed project. This, in turn, generates a willingness to experiment.

There are many positive side effects to a super-charged art program, to wit:
- greater small muscle control
- improved ability to follow auditory + visual directions
- expanded powers of observation; and
- a better self-image.

In some cases where children had serious academic and social problems, success in drawing has been a first step toward a solution.

A WORD OF CAUTION: Throw caution to the wind and ENJOY!

Helpful Hints for Teacher

Why are they so quiet?

It really works!

Why doesn't my drawing look like the one in the book?

1. You may draw these lessons <u>directly</u> on the glass of your overhead projector with overhead pens and then wipe off with a damp rag. (Do <u>not</u> use pens with permanent ink!)
2. Children must have a clear view of the screen and be encouraged to listen attentively.
3. Be conscious of the vocabulary that can be developed in each lesson.
4. Turn off the projector to recall children's attention.
5. Pick out of each lesson what works for you. Each unit has a drawing lesson, poetry, language art ideas, suggested readings, science facts, bulletin boards and 3-D art lessons.

CONTENTS

Caterpillar Capers
Ready....Set

Produce the drawings in steps on an overhead projector or chalkboard as the child follows on his paper.

Keep talking as you draw.

> What shape am I beginning with?
> I begin my line on the left and go across the page.
> Draw a small circle inside the larger one.
> This line is a diagonal.

Develop descriptive vocabulary related to each animal that has been highlighted by reading the class the suggested poetry and literature selections.

Encourage children to draw LARGE enough to fill the paper.

Drawing Steps

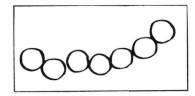 Draw circles from left _to→_ right.
Segments move _up_ and _down._
Circles are the same size.

 Facial Expression: button nose ∘
sleepy eye with drooping lid 👁
grinning mouth in profile ↵

 Each segment needs a foot.
Is he barefoot or booted?

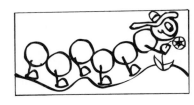 Add a floppy hat and fragrant flower.
The trail begins on the left and swells
up and down to meet his feet.

 **DESIGN IT** ➔

Is your caterpillar: striped, polka dots, wavy, zig zag, crossed, diagonal, eclectic

 Got any bright IDEAS?

So now you've drawn a caterpillar.
Now what? How about....

 Outlining with black

Add the background

Color the fellow brightly

POST TEST Follow up the next day by asking children to
draw a  looking for his lunch.

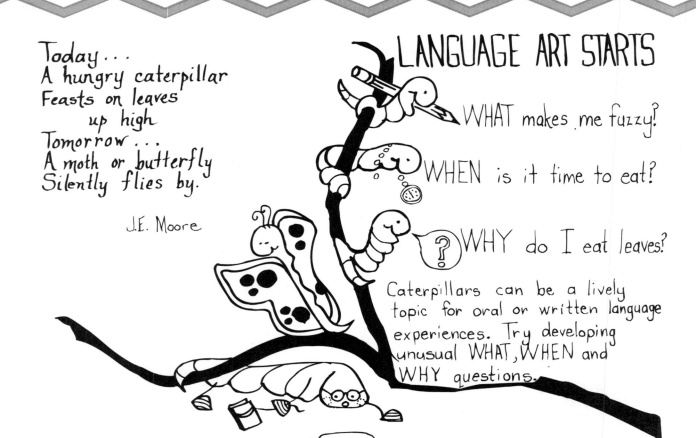

Today...
A hungry caterpillar
Feasts on leaves
    up high
Tomorrow...
A moth or butterfly
Silently flies by.

J.E. Moore

LANGUAGE ART STARTS

WHAT makes me fuzzy?

WHEN is it time to eat?

WHY do I eat leaves?

Caterpillars can be a lively topic for oral or written language experiences. Try developing unusual WHAT, WHEN and WHY questions.

Books for Fun

Down the River Without A Paddle
    by Robert and Claire West
Childrens Press
Publishing Enterprises, Inc.
Large pictures with short phrases on each page. Tells of a caterpillar's adventures on the way to becoming a butterfly. You may want your class to paint watercolor butterflies after sharing this book.
    Terry and the Caterpillar
        by Millicent E. Selsam
        Pictures by Arnold Lobel
    Harper and Row
An easy reading story full of facts on raising caterpillars at home.

Books for Facts

    I Like Caterpillars
        by Gladys Conklin
        Pictures by Barbara Lotham
    Holiday House
Shows pictures and describes various types of caterpillars as they grow to cocoon and chrysalis stages.
    Caterpillars
        by Dorothy Sterling
        Pictures by Winifred Lubell
    Doubleday and Co., Inc.
Facts on growth of caterpillars. Where to find and raise them. Also, information on silk worms and garden pests.

Caterpillar Facts

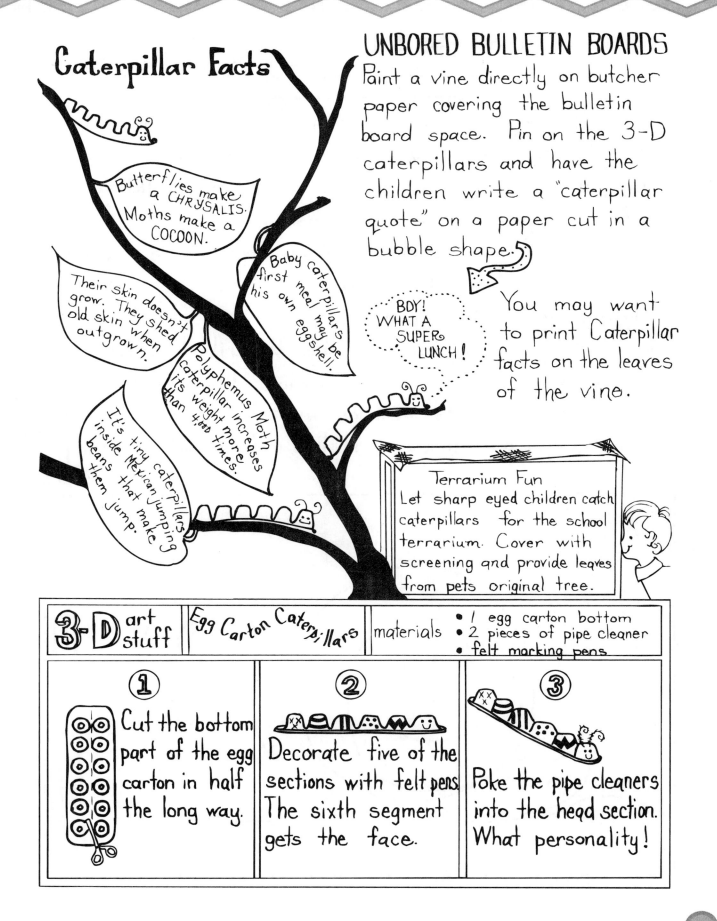

Butterflies make a CHRYSALIS. Moths make a COCOON.

Baby caterpillar's first meal may be his own eggshell.

Their skin doesn't grow. They shed old skin when outgrown.

Polyphemus Moth Caterpillar increases its weight more than 4,000 times.

It's tiny caterpillars inside Mexican jumping beans that make them jump.

BOY! WHAT A SUPER LUNCH!

UNBORED BULLETIN BOARDS

Paint a vine directly on butcher paper covering the bulletin board space. Pin on the 3-D caterpillars and have the children write a "caterpillar quote" on a paper cut in a bubble shape.

You may want to print Caterpillar facts on the leaves of the vine.

Terrarium Fun
Let sharp eyed children catch caterpillars for the school terrarium. Cover with screening and provide leaves from pets original tree.

3-D art stuff — Egg Carton Caterpillars

materials
- 1 egg carton bottom
- 2 pieces of pipe cleaner
- felt marking pens

① Cut the bottom part of the egg carton in half the long way.

② Decorate five of the sections with felt pens. The sixth segment gets the face.

③ Poke the pipe cleaners into the head section. What personality!

Snail Trails

Where to start...

Direct the drawing lesson on the overhead projector by drawing directly on the glass with an overhead projector pen. You may also use the chalkboard effectively with these lessons.

The class follows each step on their large drawing paper. It helps to encourage them to sketch lightly with their pencils.

Every shape you draw can be described. Lines can be curvy, wavy, long, longer, etc. This can be a language lesson as well as art. It is designed to equally develop language skills and visual awareness.

Drawing Steps

 Draw the large circle in the center of the paper. Begin the spiral ◎ on the bottom of the circle and roll inward.

 Now sketch in the head ⌒ and tail ⌐. Remember to tell the children that their drawing doesn't have to be identical to yours.

 All we need here is `personality`. Our snail has his basic parts, so now we can diversify. Facial features: or ?

 Begin on the left hand side and add the slotted line for the snail's trail. It can go up, over, around or anywhere.

 Let's think about where this snail is spending the afternoon. Now add your ideas to your drawing so it reflects YOU.

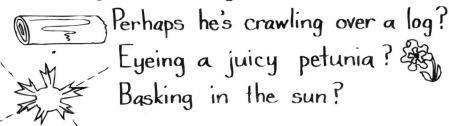 Perhaps he's crawling over a log? Eyeing a juicy petunia? Basking in the sun?

POST TEST | The child is to follow up the next day by drawing a snail upside down on a leaf.

People call me pokey
Because I move so slow
But if you had just
    one foot
How fast would YOU go?

J.E. Moore

SNAIL
TALES

Cut writing paper
into a round snail shape.
Paste it on a 12"x18" piece
of white construction paper.
Write a "snail tale" on
the shell shaped paper.
Use crayons to draw
snails head, tail and
the background.

How would you move
with one foot?

Snail Vocabulary is a must: dawdle, slink, pokey, amble, creep, crawl, etc.

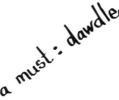

How is this for a
discussion starter?

Some people eat
snails!
Would you?

A "snail taste snack" at school would
never be forgotten!

Snail Books

Snails
by Dorothy Childs Hogner
Pictures by Nils Hogner
Thomas Y. Cromwell Co.
This book covers parts of a snail's
body, reproduction, behavior, enemies
and how to keep as pets.

The Biggest House
by Leo Lionni
Pantheon Books
The tale of a little snail determined
to have the most beautiful shell in
the world. Primary

Snail, Where Are You?
by Tomi Ungerer
Harper and Row
A good book for K or 1st grade.
No story, just delightful pictures
using a snail shell as part of
some item on each page.

Snails
by Herbert S. Zim + Lucretia Krantz
Pictures by René Martin
William Morrow + Co.
Discusses land and sea snails.
Delightful illustrations!

Snail Facts

Some snails are as small as a thimble; some have 5 pound shells.

Snails have been around for millions of years.

A gland on the foot secretes a slime which facilitates movement.

Snails cannot hear or make sound.

They are found everywhere: mountains, valleys and oceans.

Detect changes in light but not form.

UNBORED BULLETIN BOARDS

Snail's Trail of SLICK Work

Snail's shell is cut from big brown bag.
The "trail" is twisted saran wrap.
The caption is printed on butcher paper
Pin up children's work along trail.

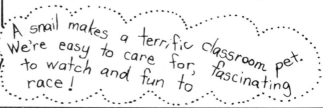

A snail makes a terrific classroom pet. We're easy to care for, fascinating to watch and fun to race!

 **3-D art stuff**  Paper Snails

materials

- Construction paper strips 2" wide in brown (18", 12", 8" long) and yellow (15" long)
- Pipe Cleaners (2 per snail — one inch)
- Paste, crayons and scissors
- One 9 x 12" green paper

directions

This lesson may be varied to fit the abilities of your class. For young children, the papers may be pre-cut or done on a ditto master and run on white art paper.

Older children could use rulers to measure strips.

Some children would enjoy decorating strips with zig-zags, polka-dots and stripes before pasting circles.

① Form the brown strips into circles.
8" strip   12" strip   18" strip
Paste

② Paste the brown circles inside one another.
← Paste at base

③ Cut yellow strip for snail body. Crayons create face.
Cut on......

④ Curl the head and tail on a pencil.

⑤ Paste the shell in the center of body.

⑥ Paste on the pipe cleaner antennae.

⑦ Paste entire snail on the green 9 x 12 paper. Draw some luscious leaves!

Turtle Topics

The Set Up

By now the students in your class know how to follow and sketch as you lead on the overhead or chalkboard.

Remember to keep talking as you draw. You are developing creative vocabulary and exciting science facts as you teach the children how to produce the animal's basic shape on paper.

The creative instincts in your children will take these basics and strike out in many different directions. You'll find this is only the beginning!

This lesson introduces what it means to draw a figure in profile.

Continue to encourage drawings large enough to fill the paper.

Drawing Steps

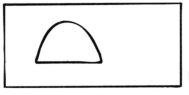 Begin with a straight line below the center of the paper and off center to the left. Draw a large /hill\ above the line.

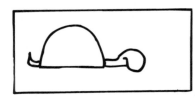 Turtles head now appears on the right and the somewhat bent tail on the left. Proportions here are flexible; don't fret!

 We are drawing the PROFILE of this turtle; so only two paddle-like feet appear His toes ᴜᴜ add interest and design.

 Profile facial expressions may vary. Pick one!

eyes ✦ ◉ ◖   eyebrows ∧ ∿ ⌃

smile frown   cheeks ⋰ ◎ ⊜

 Turtle's shell can have any pattern.

  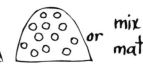 or mix + match

 Got any bright IDEAS Now the children should be encouraged to add some finishing touches.

⊔ a jaunty hat   a bouquet in his mouth

🐦 a bird nesting on his shell

| POST TEST | Follow up soon with a draw your own turtle lesson just to practice some different shell designs. |

Turtles

Little Turtle's home
Is never far away
He carries it along
As he goes about his day.

As little turtle grows
His house grows too
It fits him as well
As a shoe fits you.

J.E. Moore

Turtle Stories

LANGUAGE ART STARTS

Challenge Students to Answer Questions

See how many animals with a shell you can name in one minute. Can you draw them?

How are snails and turtles alike? How are they different?

uhm

well

Use a dictionary or encyclopedia to discover the difference between turtle and tortoise.

?

Something New for Taco

by
Jane Castellanos
Drawings by
Bernard Garbutt
Golden Gate Jr.

Adventures of a desert tortoise when it rains. Primary

Devin and Goliath

by
Mary B. Christian
Drawings by
Normand Cartier
Addison-Wesley

A little boy catches an old turtle and puts him in a cage. He releases him finally to be free. Primary

Turtles

by
Wilfred S. Bronson
Harcourt,
Brace + World

A good source of information for primary teachers. Older children can use it as a research source.

What Is A Turtle?

by
Gene Darby
Pictures by
Lucy and John
Hawkinson
Benefic Press

Many colorful pictures the turtle lifecycle and eating habits. Primary

Let's Get Turtles

by
Milicent E. Selsam
Drawings by
Arnold Lobel
Harper + Row

A Science I Can Read Book. Easy reading and written to give many facts on care of turtles in story form.

Turtle Facts

Box Turtle has a shell so strong it can support 200 times its own weight.

Some turtles live over 100 years.

Turtles have NO TEETH!

Turtles bury their eggs in holes on land.

Alligator Snapper Turtle has a long pink ridge on its tongue to attract fish. He stays on the bottom of the pond with his mouth open until a fish appears. Then SNAP!

Turtles may weigh 500 pounds.

Some turtle eggs are edible.

UNBORED BULLETIN BOARDS

You make me feel swift!

This makes for a happy place to rest your eyes during the day. Children's daily work is pinned on the turtle's shell. It builds self esteem in the students and is a great interest getter. Another option is to place "turtle facts" in each section of the shell so that it can be instructive as well as attractive.

3-D art stuff — Turtle on a String

materials
- 2 paper plates (Size is optional.)
- 6 egg carton cups — Cut egg cup off at dotted line.
- 25 inches of string or yarn
- construction paper scraps
- scissors, glue, crayons, hole punch

directions
This lesson uses materials readily available in classrooms. The result is an endearing turtle that can be pulled along the ground just like a real pet. The lesson can be adapted to all levels.

① Cut legs and tail from scrap paper and glue on edge of plate.
leg leg 4"x2" + tail 3"x1" inside

② Paste 2nd plate over the top.
Plate 2
Plate 1

③ The head is a 2"x6" paper strip. Fold in ½, draw eyes and mouth with crayons. Glue on plate.

④ Glue egg carton cups on turtle's shell.

⑤ NOW: paint him with tempera if you wish or just punch a hole in the plate under his chin and add a pull string. He will follow anywhere!

Frog Funnies

Frog offers a good lesson in change of facial expression. The movement of eyes and mouth are easy to affect and they create a new feeling each time. Movement can also be simulated by minor changes in feet positions.

As you work on the overhead projector or chalkboard you are developing an adorable character to use in creative writing stories or perhaps even a "comic strip" will evolve around his escapades.

This lesson also develops simple perspective concepts.

① Objects in distance appear smaller.

② Distant objects will be closer to the top of paper.

Comparative adjectives like large, larger, largest are useful here.

Drawing Steps

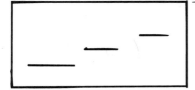 Three horizontal lines have graduated lengths. The longest one is closer to the bottom of the page because it is nearest.

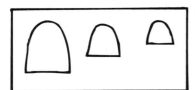 Now we have three hills drawn over the lines. They appear to recede because of size differences and placement on page.

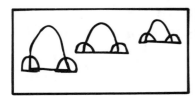 Frogs' energetic jumping legs are formed by smaller hills drawn at the base of the larger one.

 The bulbous eyes perch above a broad smile. Facial expressions vary easily and inventively!

 Frogs smaller front legs help to stabilize on hazardous landings. They have four toes. His webbed back feet are ready to jump.

 What's your frog up to?

 Resting upon a lily pad?

 Hopping around in search of BUGS!

 Snuggled in for a long winter's nap.

POST TEST Draw a progression of frogs with their legs in a new position each time to create movement.

LANGUAGE ART STARTS

Frogs
leaping away with
smooth and shiny skin

Toads
hopping along
are frog's "bumpy" kin

J.E. Moore

Frog went a courtin and he did ride

I love FROGGIE COMICS

Who	Problem	Solution
	WOW HELP	?

This is a basic lesson to help children **THINK** through a story plot. Give each child a ditto showing three boxes labeled: Who, Problem + Solution. Using a frog as the Who, have the children develop an exciting Problem and a corresponding Solution. They illustrate the strip and use bubbles to provide dialogue. Older children may then want to go on to a more detailed comic strip using more boxes.

Frog Books

Frog + Toad Are Friends
by
Arnold Lobel
Harper + Row

Easy to read misadventures of Frog and Toad.

The Frog Prince
retold by
Edith Tarcon
illustrated by
James Marshall
Four Winds Press

A retelling of Grimm's Fairy tale of the selfish princess and the frog who is really a prince.

The Frog In The Well
by
Alvin Tresselt
illustrated by
Roger Duvoisin
Lothrop, Lee + Shepard

The story of a frog living at the bottom of a well. The frog is forced out into the wide world when the well dries up.

Let's Find Out About Frogs
by
Corinne J. Naden
illustrated by
Jerry Lang
Franklin Watts, Inc.

A fascinating and clear investigation of facts about frogs.

Frog and Toad
by
Herbert S. Zim
illustrations by
Joy Buba
William Morrow + Co.

This book is older but nicely illustrated and clearly written. Compares toad and frog similarities and differences.

Frog Facts :

Frogs are amphibians. (They live part of the time in water and part of the time on land.)

They are cold-blooded.

Frogs hibernate in winter.

Tongue is attached to front of mouth and is sticky.

They help man by eating insects.

Baby frogs are called tadpoles or polliwogs.

Frogs have <u>no</u> necks.

Largest frogs grow to 10 inches.

Frogs have smooth, moist skin.

Toads have dry, rough, bumpy skin and larger eyes.

UNBORED BULLETIN BOARDS

Hungry frog <u>won't</u> be overlooked on your bulletin board. His body is simply formed from green paper following the form in the drawing lesson. Make him as big as your bulletin board allows.

body, hind legs, eyes, feet

His tongue is a strip of crepe paper. The insects are formed from circles.

body, wings, paper antennae

The title is cut out of black paper.

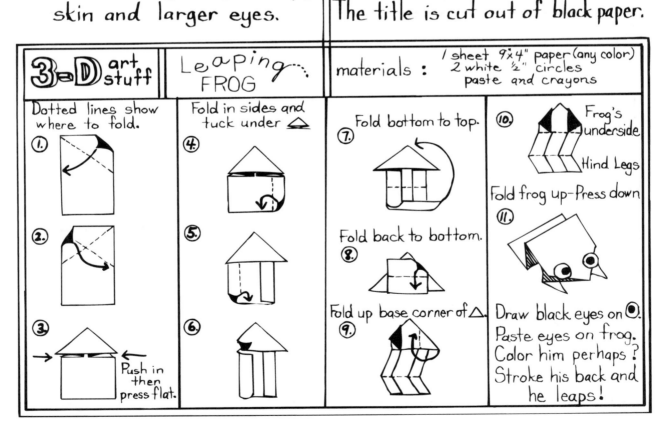

3-D art stuff

Leaping FROG

materials : 1 sheet 9"x4" paper (any color) 2 white ½" circles paste and crayons

Dotted lines show where to fold.
1.
2.
3. Push in then press flat.

Fold in sides and tuck under △
4.
5.
6.

Fold bottom to top.
7.
Fold back to bottom.
8.
Fold up base corner of △
9.

10. Frog's underside — Hind Legs — Fold frog up-Press down
11. Draw black eyes on ◎. Paste eyes on frog. Color him perhaps? Stroke his back and he leaps!

Crocodile Wiles

(Here we go again......)

Before you begin this lesson be sure you know the differences seperating the crocodile from the alligator. There is always a child who has it memorized! The crocodile fact section will help you defend yourself.

This directed drawing lesson again emphasizes:

- Sketching lightly with pencil.
- Drawing large figures that fill the page.
- The development of descriptive vocabulary.

The crocodile's zig-zagged tail and snout, the swamp grass in the background and cross hatching relief on his back all provide good design elements for adding interest and variety into the completed drawing.

Drawing Steps

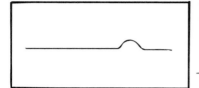
Begin on the left side below the midline of the paper.
The hill rises up just after passing center.

The zig-zagged tail has larger "zags" than the jaw in our profile view.
The ferocious jaws are mellowed by a sleepy eye.

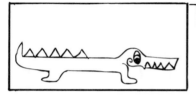
The smile curls around below the eye.
A powerful tail points skyward and two sturdy feet complete the basic form.

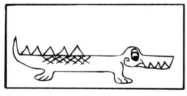
His webbed toes are visible in both front and rear.
The cross-hatching adds a sense of roughness.

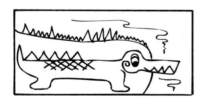
The background possibilities are fun!

a swampy shore   tall grass   water swirls

Got any bright IDEAS?

Is your crocodile looking for a tasty fish snack?

Does your crocodile have a bird on his head?

POST TEST
Follow up by having children independently draw crocodile basking in the sun.

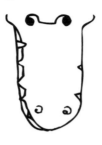 

LANGUAGE ART STARTS

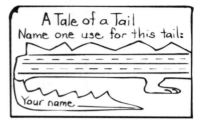

A Tale of a Tail
Name one use for this tail:

Your name _____

Alligator has a broad, broad nose

Crocodile's is thin

But both of them are dangerous

When they begin to grin

J.E. Moore

What does crocodile need that tremendous tail for anyhow? After reading factual books to the class on crocodile habits, encourage them to name as many possible uses as they can. Ideas may vary from fact to fiction and may even lead to full length escapades rather than the one line provided on above ditto.

> Crocodile Books ⬇

Tale of a Crocodile by Ann Kirn W.W. Norton + Co.	**A Crocodile's Tail** by Jose and Ariane Aruego Scholastic Books	**Lyle and the Birthday Party** by Bernard Waber Houghton-Mifflin	**Reptiles Do The Strangest Things** by Leonora + Arthur Hornblow illustrated by Michael K. Firth Random House	**Alligators and Crocodiles** by Herbert S. Zim illustrated by James Gordon Irving William Morrow + Co.
An old folktale from the Congo, in which Rabbit and his family outwit the selfish crocodile. Primary	A Philipinne folk story of a boy who rescues a crocodile. Then the boy is rescued by a monkey from the hungry crocodile.	A family's pet crocodile becomes unhappy because he has never had a birthday party. Primary	An easy to read science book. It covers many reptiles, but has an excellent chapter on crocodiles and alligators.	This is an older book, but explains about the habits of crocodiles in a clear style. Good for teacher information or intermed.

Crocodile Facts:

Crocodiles are largest reptiles today.
Most reptiles are silent, but
  crocodiles make one of the loudest
  sounds in the animal kingdom.
Only one kind is found in U.S.A.
  It lives in Florida.
Crocodiles and Alligators are
  much alike BUT.....
    Alligators have broad, rounder
    heads. ⊃
    Crocodile's head is narrow and
    pointed. ⊃ His eyes stick
    up farther and he has fewer
    teeth. His teeth are longer
    and sharper!

UNBORED BULLETIN BOARDS

Your good stories keep me afloat!

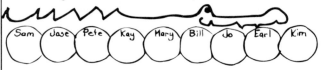

Sam · Jase · Pete · Kay · Mary · Bill · Jo · Earl · Kim

This is a good way to display work
in your room. The alligator is
cut from a green strip of butcher
paper. ▬▬▬▬ Add his
eye and teeth with a felt pen.
The bouyant bubbles are cut from
blue construction paper –
The child's papers may be pinned
in the circle for display. Their
name is put in by black felt pen.
The title is cut from black paper.

3-D art stuff ‖ Bumpy ᴬCrocodile

materials
green construction paper
  2 pieces 4"x 18"
  1 piece 4"x 4"
white construction paper 4"x 4"
crayons, paste, and scissors

① Put 2 large green pieces together:

✂ cut 2   bend up

Now fold top paper back and forth:

Now cut tail and paste together.

② small green paper for the legs

round off end
of all 4 legs then paste in place

③ white paper for eyes and teeth

→ ⬭ → ◉ → 👁 eye

→ ▭ ✂ → paste ▽ tooth

Paste eyes
and teeth on
crocodile's head.
You may put a
fish in his
mouth too.

Mouse Mischief

Try this one!

By now your overhead projector pen may need replacing.
   You've been using it a lot. If you're using a chalkboard,
   I hope you're not overcome with dust.
This lesson offers an opportunity to develop several
   language skills: • more descriptive vocabulary (petite, cautious)
                    • rhyming words (mouse-house, mice-nice)
                    • plurals (mouse-mice, goose-geese, foot-feet)
                    • cat and mouse adventure tales
We will give attention in this lesson to differentiating the
   foreground from the background.
The use of "wiggle" lines will help lend movement
   to mischievous mouse.

Drawing Steps

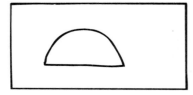 Begin with a horizontal line just off to the left of center. ——
Follow with a hill above the line. ⌒

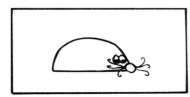 Add one circle on the right corner for a twitchy nose, two circles above the nose for tiny eyes and six curly whiskers.

 Two large circles form mouse's ears. Discuss how a profile view allows you to see the inside of only the left ear. Crosshatching gives depth.

 A twisty tail is a must! ∿
Wiggle lines give illusion of movement.
His legs move and bend; vary position for fun.

 Distinguish background from foreground by drawing a horizontal line behind mouse.
A hill on that line creates a mouse hole.

 Now children may add finishing touches.
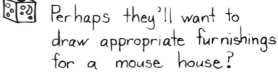 Want to make mouse into MICE?   Perhaps they'll want to draw appropriate furnishings for a mouse house?

POST TEST Follow-up soon by drawing mouse having a nibble of his favorite swiss cheese.

Meese? Mouses? Mice?

One is just a little mouse

Scurrying around the yard
or house

But when more than one
I chance to see

I'm confused!
What should it be?

J.E. Moore

Let's Talk Traps

What would you want to trap?

Would you invent your own
special trap? Describe it!

Where would you leave the
trap?

How would you bait the trap?

Have you ever been "trapped"?

MICE BOOKS

Frederick
by Leo Lionni
Pantheon Books
While most mice are storing up
food for winter, Frederick stores
up colors and words for when
the grey days of winter come.

Sing Little Mouse
by Aileen Fisher
illustrated by Symeon Shimin
Thomas Y. Crowell Co.
Story of a boy's search for
a singing mouse. Written in verse.
Beautiful illustrations.

Mouse and Company
by Lilo Hess
Charles Scribner's Sons
This book gives many facts about
the development and habits of the
Deer Mouse including how to keep
them for pets. Nice photographs.

The Story of Rodents
by Dorothy E. Shuttlesworth
illustrated by Lydia Rosier
Doubleday and Co., Inc.
A beautifully illustrated book of
factual information on many varieties
of rodents.

Mouse's Favorite Things

This easy to make bulletin board is fun to adapt to any area of the curriculum. It makes a great way to display children's work or it could also be used to reinforce science facts, math facts, reading vocabulary, etc. Mouse is cut from black butcher paper and the board itself is backed in mouse's favorite color— "creamy, cheesey yellow".

Mouse Puppet

Mouse Facts

- Mice are more active at night.
- Field Mice use tails for climbing and balancing.
- Meadow Mouse eats own weight in seeds every 24 hours.
- White-Footed Mouse hums in throat and thumps front paw.
- Hazel Mouse hibernates in the winter.
- Meadow Jumping Mouse can jump twelve feet.
- Mice are rodents!
- Baby Mice are born blind and hairless.

3-D art stuff

Read the "City and Country Mouse" tale and then make two of these puppets to depict the story!

materials

one 9"x12" gray construction paper
two 4"x4" gray
two 3"x3" pink
one 6"x3" black
one 6"x3" red or blue
scissors, paste and crayons

① Fold 9"x12" gray paper into thirds. Overlap and paste. Round off top for head.

   Cut on dotted line.

② Paste top of head closed. Cut ears from the 4"x4" gray and 3"x3" pink. Paste pink on gray. Cut a slit in the bottom of ears. Overlap slightly and paste for a 3-D look.

③ Cut eyes, nose, whiskers and tail from black. Paste them on and then draw the mouth and red cheeks.

④ Cut a bow-tie if you're making a "city-type" mouse, or design a neckerchief for a "country-style" mouse using red and blue paper.

Walrus Whimsy

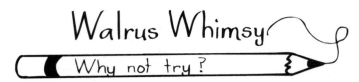

Why not try?

Walrus is easy to draw and is a unit that is enthusiastically enjoyed by children of all ages. He is a lively topic for comic art and fictitious tales of fun and daring.

The science facts about Walrus are fascinating. The idea that a body so encumbered could move with such speed is a wonder.

Follow the regular procedures for development of the drawing as well as vocabulary and fact enrichment.

Attention will be given to design concepts through the various possible patternings used for water and whisker treatments.

Be sure walrus is drawn large enough to fill the page!

Drawing Steps

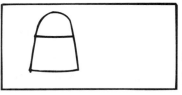
Begin with a tall hill off-center to the left.
Allow space at lower edge for his flipper.
Draw a line across the top to form head.

Add a ⌒ on the top line for a moustache.
The nose ⱽ and tusks ⎮⎮ show up next.
The bottom flipper ⌒⟋ reaches to the side.

The bulging black eyes are looking straight
    ahead at us!
The sensitive bristles form the moustache.

The Walrus rounds out into a double-
    double chin.
His side flippers are shaped like oars.

Walrus happily rests on an ice floe.
The water surrounding the floe can assume
    many designs and forms.
                                    etc.

Try outlining the wave formations with the
    cool colors: blue, green and purple.
Outline Walrus in black and color brown.

| POST TEST | Ask children to draw Walrus swimming in the water searching for clams. |

LANGUAGE ART STARTS

A bristly moustache across
his face
Great white tusks firmly
in place
Weighing a ton at the
very least
Walrus is a marvelous
beast.

J.E. Moore

Walrus is a good subject for the creation of a cinquain.
Cinquain is a five lined poem and each line follows a form:

1 One word (title)

2 Two words (describing the title)

3 Three words (describe an action)

4 Four words (expressing a feeling)

5 ONE word (referring back to title)

Practice as a group-then explore!

Walrus Books

The Walrus and The Carpenter
by
Lewis Carroll
illustrations by
Gerald Rose
E. P. Dutton + Co.

Contains all verses of the Walrus + the Carpenter plus many other poems by Lewis Carroll.

The Walrus, Giant of the Arctic
by
Kay McDearmon
Dodd, Mead + Co.

This book follows the travels of a Mother Walrus and her year old calf. Illustrated with black and white photographs.

Four Walruses
by
Lou Jacobs, Jr.
Young Scott Books

The story of four walruses from Alaska who are captured as babies and raised at Marineland in California.

Walpole
by
Syd Hoff
Harper + Row

An easy reader about the biggest and strongest Walrus of all and how he becomes leader of the herd.

Seals of the World
by
Gavin Maxwell
Constable + Co.

An excellent source for teacher research.

It's true about Walrus:

He has no outside ears.
Male tusks may be 3 feet long!
He may weigh 3000 lbs.
Lives in the arctic among icebergs.
He uses tusks to dig clams.
He has no fur but 2" thick skin,
　　and 6" of blubber.
Has about 400 bristles in his
　　moustache-serves sensory
　　function and helps shovel food in.
Can swim up to 15 mph and run
　　as fast as a man.
Hind flippers rotate foreward so
　　walrus can run very fast.
Baby rides on mother's back.

3-D art stuff Walrus Puppet

materials
Paper : 9"x12" light brown
　　　　 8"x3"　　dark brown
　　　　 2"x3"　 white
8 flat toothpicks (or 4 broken in half)
paste, glue, scissors, crayons

① Fold light brown paper into thirds.
　 Overlap and paste.
　 Round off top for head.
　 Paste top of head closed.

② Fold 8"x3" dark brown paper and cut
　 on fold lines. [a ¦ b ¦ c]
　　 a = moustache Round off corners
　　　　and cut small curve [.....] → ⌒
　　 b,c = flippers [___] → ▱

UNBORED BULLETIN BOARDS

Sharing Center

Arrange a table below this board so
the children can display articles or
books they've brought to school to
share. You can jot down a sentence
for each item shared on a tag
sentence strip and lay it on the
table. Want to develop a discussion
use of quotation marks?

John said, "This is my new spaceman."

Tara said, "This lava rock is light."

"I wanted you to see this book," said Gus.

③ Fold 2"x3" white paper and cut on
　 the fold line.
　 Round off one end for tusks.

④ Assemble puppet

Paste on　　Draw eyes　　Paste on
moustache　and nostrils　tusks and flippers.
　　　　　　in black crayon.

⑤ GLUE toothpicks onto moustache
　 for bristles.

　 Allow glue to dry before using.

　　　 Now....
　　　　　　 enjoy him!

The bear can be adapted by children to draw and create original stories and illustrations about the many popular bear characters in literature and films.

Science and vocabulary development can benefit from a discussion of hibernation and other bear habits.

This lesson continues to develop visual concepts involved in simple perspective.

Texture is explored here with the lines used to simulate fur.

Children need to be reminded that sketching means using the pencil with a very light and carefree touch.

Bears need to be LARGE to be effective.

Drawing Steps

Begin with a centered horizontal line. —
Add a hill above the line. ⌒
A circle sits over the hill. ◯

Bear's ears are double circles. ◎ ◎
Another hill forms the tummy. ⌂
The legs and feet extend to the lower edge.

An upside down hill creates the facial mask. ∪
Arms wrap around with hands clasped in front.
Add toe marks on feet.

Two sparkley eyes appear.
Also a nose that slips easily into a smile.
Create a "furry illusion" by using
zig-zags.

Draw the horizon line behind bear.
The closer tree appears larger. The distant tree is smaller.

What can individualize your drawing?
• Is bear picking a bouquet of wildflowers?
  Is bear's brother hiding behind that tree?

POST TEST   Follow-up soon by asking children to draw mother bear and her two cubs.

Bears Bears Everywhere Bears

Grizzly bears are daring and bold

Polar bears live in Arctic cold

Black bears busily search for grubs

Sun bears play with their baby cubs

Wherever you go the whole world
round

The mighty bear family can be found

J.E. Moore

LANGUAGE ART STARTS

Use the bear puppets to encourage oral creativity. There is so much to try!

• Let them recreate the Three Bears Story.
• Memorize the poem
• Have each "personal bear" describe his very favorite lunch menu.
• Answer the question: "What's the Bruin doing next winter?"

Bear Books
(only to mention a few)

Bears
by
Ruth Krauss
illustrations by
Phyllis Rowand
Harper + Row

An old but delightful picture book of rhymes for bear. Primary

Buzzy Bear Goes South
by
Dorothy Marino
Franklin Watts
Inc.

Little Bear decides to follow the birds south for the winter. He keeps returning for forgotten items until he grows tired and goes to sleep.

A Kiss For Little Bear
by
Else H. Minarik
illustrations by
Maurice Sendak
Harper Row

One of a series of easy to read stories about Little Bear. He sends his Grandmother a gift and she sends him a kiss.

Wonders of the World of Bears
by
Bernadine Bailey
Dodd, Mead + Co.

Black and white photos of bears around the world. Each chapter describes a type of bear and its habits.

The Bear Family
by
Dorothy Wood
illustrated by
Harriett
Harvey House, Inc.

Discusses general habits of North American bears. Nice pencil illustrations.

The Bare Facts Are:

Bears have 5 toes on each foot with a sharp claw on each toe.

Bears have poor eyesight but keen sense of smell and hearing.

The bear walks awkwardly; he lifts both right feet, then left.

They can run very fast for short distances.

Bears sleep during winter. They store fat under their skin for warmth and nourishment while asleep.

Bears eat many things: meat, fish, berries, grubs, ants, honey.

UNBORED BULLETIN BOARDS

I spend all winter with a book!
Winnie Who?

Try this in your library center. You may display real book jackets and change them weekly. It's also a good motivational technique to post children's stories in bear's paws. Bear may also be used with a different title to emphasize current math or language concepts. He's versatile and easy to make

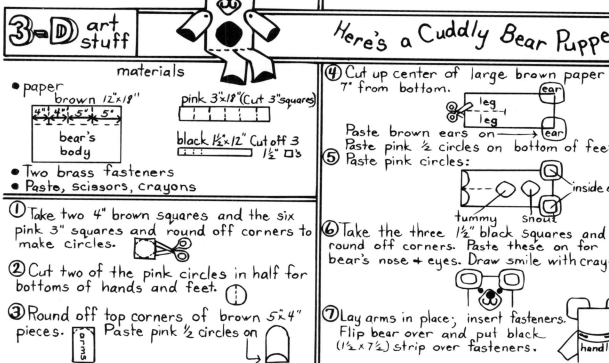

3-D art stuff

materials

- paper
  - brown 12"x18"

4"	4"	5"	5"

bear's body

  - pink 3"x18" (Cut 3"squares)
  - black 1½"x12" Cut off 3 1½" □'s
- Two brass fasteners
- Paste, scissors, crayons

① Take two 4" brown squares and the six pink 3" squares and round off corners to make circles.

② Cut two of the pink circles in half for bottoms of hands and feet.

③ Round off top corners of brown 5"x4" pieces. Paste pink ½ circles on

Here's a Cuddly Bear Puppet

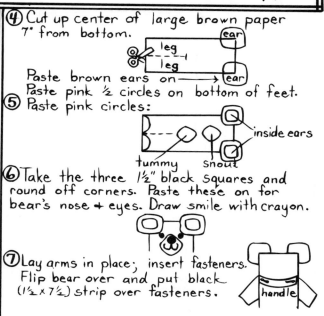

④ Cut up center of large brown paper 7" from bottom.

Paste brown ears on
Paste pink ½ circles on bottom of feet.

⑤ Paste pink circles:
inside ears
tummy   snout

⑥ Take the three 1½" black squares and round off corners. Paste these on for bear's nose + eyes. Draw smile with crayon.

⑦ Lay arms in place; insert fasteners. Flip bear over and put black (1½ x 7½) strip over fasteners.
handle

Elephant Illustrations
Begin again....

Get your overhead pen ready. This one is always a HUGE
success! Elephant prose and poetry sources abound and
children are very responsive to creating stories and
illustrations on this subject. A unit on Elephants
can utilize reading, language arts, music, art, math
and science topics for a unified study enjoyed by all.
We continue to emphasize: • sketching lightly with pencil
                          • draw large enough to fill paper
                          • utilize descriptive vocabulary
This lesson will also concentrate on important directional
   instructions and vocabulary: above, below, over, under, etc.

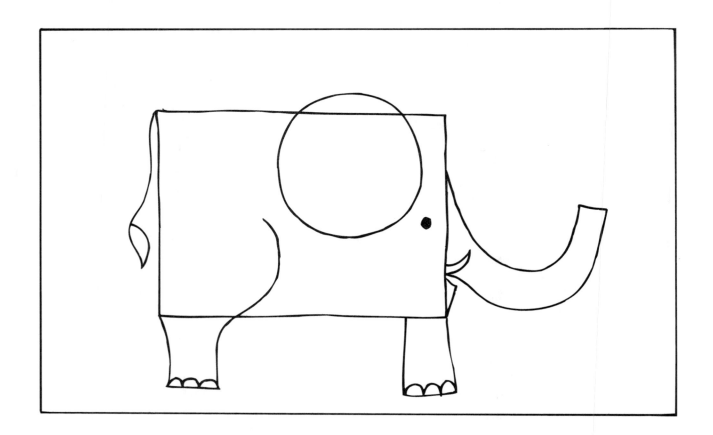

Drawing Steps

Draw a large rectangle.
It should be offset toward the left side of the paper.

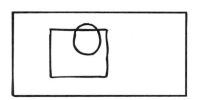

A circle forms elephant's ear. Only one ear is visible because of profile view. Circle is in upper right hand corner.

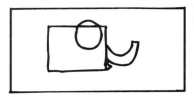

My trunk swings upward looking for peanuts. Where is yours? Variety allowed!

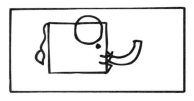

A small eye appears below the large floppy ear and a tusk beside the trunk.
A tail ready to swish brings up the rear.

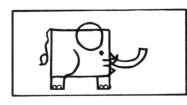

Two short stubby legs are drawn on the bottom of the rectangle. The rear leg begins high on the left. Toenails add interest.

Where does your elephant live?

in a jungle | in the zoo | with a circus

POST TEST

Follow-up tomorrow by asking students to draw an elephant reaching for a delicious peanut.

Gray
Wrinkled
  Saggy
    Skin
That's the cover
  an elephant's in.

J.E. Moore

Way down south
    where bananas grow
A grasshopper stepped
    on an elephant's toe.
The elephant cried
    with tears in his eyes
Pick on somebody
    your own size.

Anonymous

LANGUAGE ART STARTS

Let's write about the **2** types of

African *Asian*

I have very large ears and tusks. I have two "finger-like" tips on the end of my trunk to help me pick up things.

I have small ears. I have only one "finger-like" tip, but I can still pick up objects.

Here is a TUSK-FULL of big words to use in writing:
gargantuan enormous gigantic
immense humongous huge

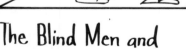

GOOD BOOKS

The Blind Men and the Elephant	retold by Lillian Quigley pictures by Janice Holland Charles Scribner's Sons	Six blind men meet an elephant. Each describes the animal from his point of view.
The Elephant's Child from Just So Stories	Rudyard Kipling pictures by Nicolas	Tells how the elephant gets his long trunk.
Elephants	Joe Wormer E.P. Dutton + Co. Inc.	Compares Asian and African elephants. Large photos.

Elephant Fact Test:

Here is a quiz to stimulate interest in the beginning of the unit. Children indicate choice of answer by- thumbs up for true, thumbs down for false.

What do _YOU_ know about elephants?
TRUE or **FALSE**

F 1. Most elephants come from Africa.

F 2. A man can outrun an elephant.

F 3. Elephants are the largest of all animals.

F 4. An elephant's trunk is its best weapon.

T 5. Tusks grow back if they are broken.

F 6. An elephant's trunk has only one use.

T 7. An elephant's skin is an inch or more thick.

T 8. Elephants can't run or gallop.

F 9. Elephants are afraid of mice.

T 10. An elephant can smell water three miles away.

UNBORED BULLETIN BOARDS

YOU are a huge success.

Make this fanciful elephant head out of the classified ad section of your newspaper. Cut the paper to fit the dimensions of your board. The backing should be a bright color to provide contrast. Make the "bubble" on white paper. The cheeks are red circles. The trunk is a strip of paper pleated like an accordian. Now pin up children's work on his ears.

3-D art stuff | Stand-up Elephant Parade ....

① 9" / 12"

Pick a color you like of 9"x12" construction paper.

Fold it in half.

②

Make 1 cut for the trunk. Cut out a half circle on the bottom and round off the top right hand corner.

③

Use the half circle scraps for the two ears. Use the rounded off corners for the tail. Paste on.

④

Draw eyes and toe nails with crayons or felt pens. Fold up feet each a ½". Stand him on his own four feet!

Make several in different colors and sizes of paper. Crayons can also add bright circus blankets.

Giraffe Acts

You won't have any trouble convincing children to draw
   large and fill the paper on this one!

The "giraffe trio" offers you a choice. You may begin by
   drawing only one giraffe or they may be drawn in
   a series to simulate the motions of bending down.
   Children enjoy creating flip books to show this
   action speeded up. Giraffe is beautiful whether he
   is moving or standing still.

Design possibilities may be discussed when considering the
   way Giraffe's spots seem to "just fit together".

The lanky giraffe also offers humorous veins to explore
   in drawing and story-telling.

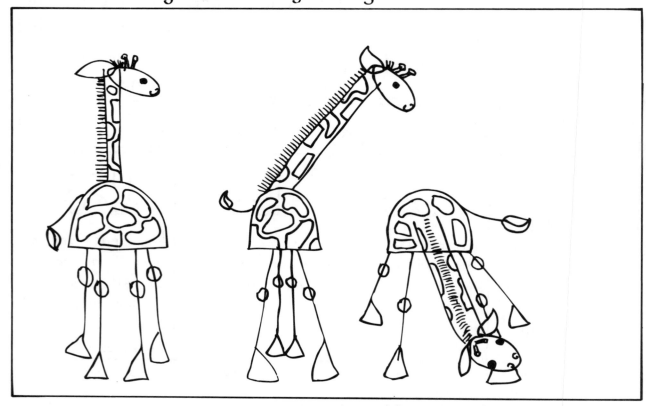

Drawing Steps

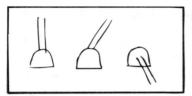

Begin with the circles spaced across the paper.
The neck columns reach almost to top edge.

The oval heads may turn other directions.
Giraffe's legs are shown in various positions.
Bend and move them in your own way.

The rear legs lend a comic appeal, or is it just those bony knees?
The fringe is evenly spaced sticks. ||||||||||

The ear is shaped like a leaf. ⬭ You may choose to show both ears in your pose.
The nose and mouth lend such character.

His horns are a great addition and a swishing tail may appear anywhere!
Giraffe spots have many contours.

Now where can YOU go with your drawing?

I'm stunning outlined in black!

Where can a guy get a juicy tree and drink of river water.

POST TEST Follow up by having class draw giraffe on a piece of construction paper cut to 6"x 18" TALL.

LANGUAGE ART STARTS

He swiftly moves across the plains

He silently stands in the falling rains

Or reaches for tender shoots and leaves

That grow in the tops of the tallest trees

These are some of the interesting ways

The gentle giraffe passes his days.

J.E. Moore

Category Game

Divide class into 2 teams. Supply each child with a magazine and scissors. The teams are given a 20 minute limit to cut out pictures of

SPOTTED THINGS!

The team with the most examples wins. Then everyone pastes their findings on a large chart and labels their discoveries. (Freckled people excel at this task.)

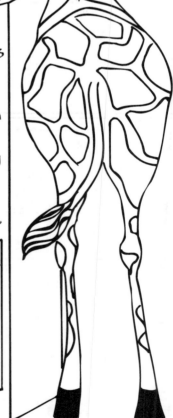

Giraffe Books

Mr. Tall and Mr. Small	Cecily G and the 9 Monkeys	Giraffe the Silent Giant	Giraffe Lives In Africa
by Barbara Brenner	by Hans A. Rey	by Miriam Schlein	by Gladys Conklin
illustrated by Tomi Ungerer	Houghton-Mifflin	illustrated by Betty Fraser	illustrated by M. Kalmenoff
Young Scott Co.	Adventures occur when a lonesome giraffe becomes friends with nine homeless monkeys.	Four Winds Press	Holiday House
Book is in rhyme. Giraffe and Mouse quarrel over whether it is better to be tall or small.		For teacher information or intermediate students. Everything you wanted to know about giraffes.	The experiences of a baby giraffe growing up written in story form. Intermediate

Giraffe Facts:

They are the tallest mammals.

Some can reach the height of eighteen feet!

Their bodies are short, the height comes from long necks and legs.

Giraffe's neck has only seven vertebrae.

Front legs are longer than back.

They are native to Africa, south of the sahara and live in open bush country.

Giraffes browse upon trees.

A full gallop = 30 m.p.h.

<u>Do</u> make sounds, but are seldom heard.

UNBORED BULLETIN BOARDS

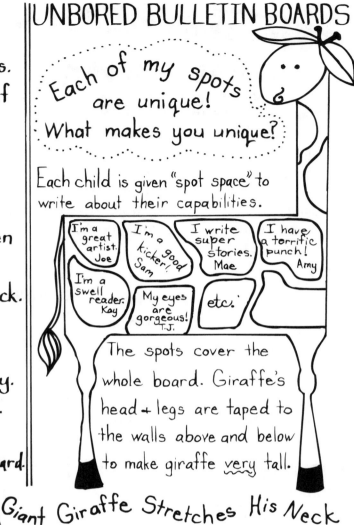

Each of my spots are unique! What makes you unique?

Each child is given "spot space" to write about their capabilities.

I'm a great artist. Joe

I'm a good kicker! Sam

I write super stories. Mae

I have a terrific punch! Amy

I'm a swell reader. Kay

My eyes are gorgeous! T.J.

etc.

The spots cover the whole board. Giraffe's head + legs are taped to the walls above and below to make giraffe <u>very</u> tall.

3-D art stuff

• materials •

paper –
  one yellow 12"x18" (backing)
  one yellow 10"x 4" (neck)
  one brown 6"x 9" (tree+spots)
  green tissue in 1" squares
  one black 1"x 12"
paste, scissors, crayons

① Cut tree trunk off edge of brown paper. Paste it on left edge of large yellow.

② Crush tissue paper squares over eraser end of pencil and paste on for leaves.

Giant Giraffe Stretches His Neck

③ Draw giraffe's head and neck on narrow yellow strip. Outline in black and draw in giraffe's face. Cut out ⟿

④ Cut black strip. 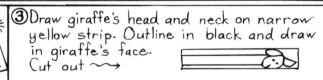 ←tail

mane   horns

Paste mane to neck and horns to the head.

⑤ Lay the neck to the tree and paste head and base of neck forming a rise like a bridge. Sketch the rest of giraffe's body directly on the yellow paper and outline with black crayon.

⑥ Cut free form brown spots and paste on body and neck of giraffe.

⑦ Draw in the background with crayons.

Take It to Your Seat
Learning Centers

Centers are a wonderful, motivating way for students to practice important skills. Here are 10 books with self-contained, portable centers. The storage system is built-in—hanger pockets, shoeboxes, or folders. Once you've made the centers, they're ready to use at any time. **$19.99 each.**

MATH

Math Centers K–1	**EMC 3020**
Math Centers 1–3	**EMC 3013**
Math Centers 4–6	**EMC 3012**

LITERACY

Early Learning Centers PreK–K	**EMC 2401**
Literacy Centers K–1	**EMC 2123**
Literacy Centers 1–3	**EMC 788**
Literacy Centers 3–4	**EMC 2124**
Language Arts Centers 4–6	**EMC 2719**

SCIENCE

Science Centers 1–2	**EMC 5002**
Science Centers 3–4	**EMC 5003**

- **Full-color materials to construct the centers**

- **Full-color and reproducible student task cards**

- **Teacher directions**

- **192 pages**

Literacy Centers—
Grades 1-3 EMC 788

Categories

Math Centers—
Grades K-1 EMC 3020

My Bug Jar

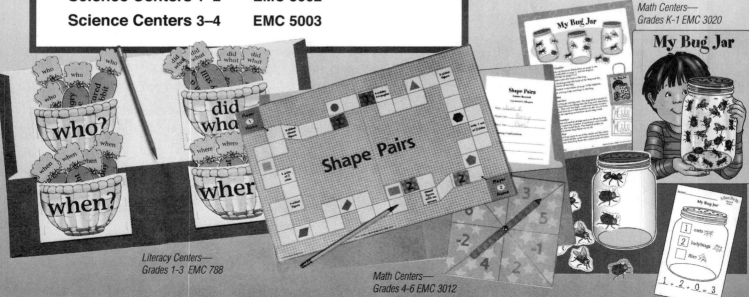

Literacy Centers—
Grades 1-3 EMC 788

Shape Pairs

Math Centers—
Grades 4-6 EMC 3012